Spaces in Time

Prose and poetry
by
Larkin Stentz

2011

Table of Contents

Larkin Stentz
P.O. Box 1229
Long Beach, WA 98631
larkin804@gmail.com

Introduction

What was thought at first to be a Christmas gift of poems for a few friends has emerged as a poetic journey of moments over 40 years.

Grateful am I for my friends who love me, wrinkles and all. To inspire me to put this collection together has offered the opportunity to reflect on the layers of my tapestry. As words in a poem by Michele Easton - Cortright expresses - "We weave our lives in many colors..." so within this collection are many colors within the tapestry of my life. I see them as glimpses of my emersion in the layers of life's mystery. Some glide over moments, seeing the textures on the surface. Some come from deeply swimming in the waters of my emotions. Still others are observations from that spiritual realm from which we receive guidance. And others, who knows?

Some poems seem to have come with one line to impart. Like "personality bound being unfolds..." is one such line that has a story all its own.

It is my hope that one of these will give you pause, to consider the colors in your tapestry.

In Joy - Larkin
12/2012

*There are deeper
rhythms that we must
dance to
other than the calendar of events
our culture prescribes.*

Night bird

The night bird calls
        deep,
from a meadow within.

Few hear
or pay any heed.

Snow and ice
        cover the ground,
The seed hears
        sleeps
        grows
        grows ready for spring.
Look
inside...
what seeds have you planted,
        forgotten?
Listen
        the night bird calls
        Will your spring bear fruit?
        Or have you forgotten
                to tend your seed?

Who among us

Who among us speaks even half a truth?

Is the earth not in crisis?
Is childbirth not a crises - mother and child both
dancing on the edge.
Earth mother is in labor now
We are the star child,
From our mother we have received
and to her we must give,
Then, then, then from this giving
We shall have everlasting peace.

Time and Space

That pregnant place
In Time and Space
Where past and future memory
meet in a vision of one
throughout eternity.

A time no place
has yet been found
To call home for this vision
to be ground.

In the air, sea, fire and soil
lie the memory
all beings - one.

The time is now
the place within
the seed grows
of one vision to begin.

Comes forth the seed
from within
the knowing soul

Breaking through the ground
Of the personality bound
being - unfolds.

Hearing the call
in an ancient tongue
it speaks...

"Live the souls desire,
create the music
dance the dance
form the vision
of the oneness all aspire."

Harmony predisposes differences.

*In a moment of silence
A million suns are born,
Which one are you?*

When all about is chaos,
A flower blooms -
Be that flower

A moment in time

A moment in time as midnight passes quietly on busy streets.
Somber reflections on the now and then of yesterday.
Becoming whole with moments in the universe is being.
Frustration is a configuration for maintaining the past, eating
leftovers day after day until they are gone - then to cook a
configuration again.
Without sadness there is no drama, no actors but especially no
roles or scripts to read - after all, how many comedies do you
know?
Laughter is love, God and oblivious harmony.
I'm so scared of being well!

Pleasures of the soul

Passion lies beneath my soft exterior friend,
I am a warrior for the pleasures of the soul.
Fantasies strip away our cloths, embracing, intertwining, waters
disintegrating the differences.
Wakefulness creeps over our recent history,
we see a new world of differences now.
The warrior sleeps,
exhausted in another attempt to satisfy the pleasure of the soul.

Striving ceases
The seed of truth unfolds
*   the differences*
*   the oneness*
Both - hands for the pleasures of the soul.

Petals Unfolding in the Light

Petals unfolding in the light
  With memories of seasons past
Warm springs that faded too soon
  Hot summers that lingered too long
Brilliant fall colors
  That seemed to last forever
Winter dreams of all things beautiful.

Petals unfolding in the light
  of our love
Bring up memories, some deep and dark
  Others high and bright.
Staying present with our light
  Looking at all the remembered seasons
   That arise
And throughout the journey
  Our light will shine
As we embrace the day
  And hold in the night
Unfolding new petals
  of delight.

Oh Hellebore

Oh Hellebore
 Gift of love and so much more...
Through snowy nights
 Your countenance bears
So at morning light
 You blossom bright and fare...

As winter's darkness wanes
 Your strength unfolds a beauty with wings...

Other colors now too appear
 A primrose, a violet, a forsythia fare
But none can compare
 To the hellebore
 A gift from my amore
 That lights my heart
 And so much more.

While Naked Standing

While naked standing at my door
Having showered and nothing more
Hung a single ripe strawberry
From the basket you made with such merry.
Gently pulling it from the vine
It came easily to be mine
Slowly melting ripe juices on my tongue
My mouth seemed to swell with sweetness when I was done.
With the strawberry made merry from the rich soil of your garden floor
I stood delighted and naked at my door
And nothing more.

You give me the pause

You give me the pause to connect
You give me the rhyme to reason
You give me truth for the telling
You give me light for the shadows
You give me mountains for the valleys
You give me the ocean for the rivers
You give me the rain for the clouds
You give me the spirit for the breath
You give me the melody for the music

You give me to me
*   and in all of this*
You give me love
*   and I am nourished.*

Stretching

*Stretching, flowers move
to the light
Soft bells of blossoms
ring in the night
Subtle fragrances
whisper soft graces
And the fairies sing
of sweet Carol
gardener of delight.*

Don't tell the sun not to shine...

Don't tell the sun not to shine
      Because you're having trouble with your mind...
Don't tell the river not to run
      Because your life has only just begun...
Don't tell the forest not to grow
      When the hair on your head is all you have to show...
Don't tell the moon not to rise
      Because you have dark glasses over your eyes
Don't tell the wind not to blow
      Because you're growing way to slow
Don't tell the flowers not to emerge
      When it's anger in your heart that you need to purge
Don't tell me not to love
      Because it's your fear you can't rise above

The Sun Shines
The River Flows
The Forest Grows
The Moon will rise
And the Wind will blow
And the flowers will show
That love will always grow
Because love was their beginning
And
Love
Is
Neverending.

Striving ceases, the seed of truth unfolds
the differences
the oneness
both, - hands for the pleasure of the soul.

Come Watch the Crows Gather

Come watch the crows gather
From my perch among the clouds
We'll lie and spoon to warm another
As we whisper dreams we journeyed upon

Come watch the crows gather
As morning light grows its embers
Lighting sky and earth with flowing fingers
Lying still in warm embrace
Our wanting soothed by night's loving grace.

Come and watch the crows gather
With salmon and azure sky
To and fro their cedar spire
They bring on the day with a cacophonous choir

Come and watch the crows gather
As the light of a new day dawns.

Listen to the wind

Listen to the wind in the trees
I will sing to you with the breeze
Soft melodies of dancing hands
      Loving bodies lying twined on the land

The plants listen as we sing
      our love song
Laughter and delight
      find comfort in our light

Listen to the wind in the trees
I will sing to you in the breeze
Soft melodies for dancing hands
      and loving bodies lying on the land.

Embracing

Embracing as we lay
Your head on my chest
My fur cradles your face
Your fingers comb
the trees of my forest

Breathing we blend
And there is no beginning
nor end...

I love lying with you

I love lying with you in the morning
        Soft light bathing your skin
The fit of our bodies - then
        A shift, a move finds
        Oh yes
That spot that fits so nicely.

I love lying with you in the garden
        Gazing at nature's bounty
        Smelling the rich soil
        Hearing the birds and the breeze
Watching your hair catch a wind
And ride up to my face laughing
Holding, our dancing fingers
        Touching, tracing the hills and valleys
        To a rhythm all their own and...
The garden laughs with delight.
I love lying with you on the floor
        Your head on my shoulder
        Arms intertwined, hands holding
        And we laughing.
Sometimes standing and holding
        Is lying together
In the kitchen, swaying, embracing
        Turning around and stirring
        Nibbling, kissing and stirring
        Our insides and breakfast, lunch and dinner
        Oh, what a seasoning.
I love lying with you
        in the afterglow of our loving
As the embers of millions of our cells
        Sigh,
        And we breath and become breath...
I love lying with you...

Lingering and listening

The morning waves crashing
Alders budding, rustling in the wind
Early Robin announces, awake, awake
And the clear memory of your visit still lingers

Like a fragrance with vision
You saw the TV on
          there was no sound
And Pshta, a glance
not to be found.

I watched as your loving gaze
          Rolled over memories
          Our love making
          Our laughter
          The light through the windows

Your presence lingered
          As I drifted into sleep.
To wake and remember
You visited last night,
          how nice.....

(Pshta is my feline friend)

The mound

I like the mound just above
        the folds of your yoni
I imagined cupping your mound today
        while working in the garden.
I cupped you,
        You moaned, and your waters began...

With my palm I slowly did small circles
        slowly parting your lips
        exploring your tender folds
You moaned, and your waters flowed

You moaned your pleasure
        as your head leaned back
        and your eyes closed.

Words

I send out words like carrier pigeons,
Hoping for their return,
Acknowledgement of my ownership.

Come walk with me

You beckoned and said
        Come walk with me
        And I cried
I walked with you
        On the beach
        Side by side
You holding my arm
        Lovingly looking into my eyes
        You said
        Come walk with me
        And I cried
We walked and walked
        Erupting from deep within
        Sobs emerged
        Cleansing old times that had been
And you said
        Come walk with me
        And I cried.
Mile after mile
        Flowing, old pain came out
I cried, a part of me is dying
        You said, yes, it is letting go
        And I cried
Mile after mile
        Memory upon memory
        Waves releasing and joining the sea
And you said come walk with me
        And I cried
Later you beckoned,
        Come walk with me
Now we walked arm in arm seeing
Trees, iris and water hyacinth blending
And the power within grew again.
We walked and with each step
        Loving wisdom now claimed
The spaces where tears had cleansed
You beckoned
        Walk with me
        And I did
        And we grew.

Like Elephants

Like Elephants with their tusks
          gently caressing the bones
          of their departed companion

I sway, my head, back and forth
          Looking, remembering, feeling your
          Preciousness

I sense your eyes behind, alongside, with,
          part of my eyes -
Seeing your's looking at me
          with the love only your eyes can speak.
My - our eyes touch our things,
          hold them as the gifts they are...

Watching in my mind the elephants
          tender remembrances
          drawn from bone.

I can understand now
          those that hold onto ashes
          there is history there -
A tome of knowledge
          in the dust of those fibers.

I feel heavy and substantial
          As an elephant
Weight like waves
          back and forth
Passing from foot to foot
          a long tear stream
          leading from the eyes
The tusk lifting, nuzzling, turning over
          the bones
Sipping last fragrant fragments
          of loving character
Oh - were I an elephant
          how I would honor your bones
I am elephant - I honor your bones.

Six Months

So tear full yesterday
The ocean of emotion
Dissolving all my senses

No one time or place now
A handful of unmolded clay
All the feelings
> *All the tears*
> *All the fears*
> *All the rage*
> *All the love*
> > *Melding*
> *Molting*
Re modeling my soul
Into what, whom, when

Change is merging with my path
And coaxing movement
Toward some where new
Life
with and without
You

Limbo Land

Limbo land
Not old
Not young
      Ha Ha Middle aged
Not lesbian
Not gay
Widowed, alone.

The birds come every morning for feed
Trees stretch in the morning sun
Kale flowers nod yes, no, maybe

Everything sets - still
A picture which once captured a moment in time
Struggles in my mind to come alive again

No, that would truly hurt I think
Then, going on would have to start all over again.

Becalmed in this middle zone, limbo land
Not old
Not young
Widowed - alone

Maybe if I blow on the sails, whew, whew, whew, whew....

And The Owl Called His Name

We had known each other for over ten years. Our time together covered a spectrum of events and emotions from the mundane to the unbelievable.

Yet the events of our last week together were like the final coalescing of pieces of a puzzle which only came together after ten years.

Kidney failure was the diagnosis. The lost appetite, the limp, the constant sleeping were all symptoms. The clarity in the eyes remained. The looks that said so much and never failed to make their impression.

In a remote, quiet place the call came. To me it was just the calling of an owl, but to him... a calling which he answered - immediately. The answering sound came from a deep place within him. He followed the call, walking into the night. God knows how he walked, he had been bed ridden for ten days. I followed.

An old path was found, even in the dark. Funny, years earlier when we had first found this path I had remarked how it would be a good place to "crossover." And now here he was beginning his final journey.

After what seemed endless stopping and starting a pause came in our journey. Tired and not really thinking the time had come, I picked him up and carried him back.

Not two minutes had we returned when the call came again and again he answered and again he headed for the door. I surrendered to his timing now.

During the next twenty hours or so we walked, stopped, napped, walked, stopped, etc... We must have said farewell a hundred times. His eyes stayed clear and he spoke of letting go and how wonderful our friendship had been.

Sleep finally came over me and when I awoke he had crossed over. The tree where he is buried blooms with periwinkle year round now.

In the evening of the day he crossed over I was roused from sleep by screeching and the pounding of wings. For a moment, an owl was at my bedroom window. The last piece of the puzzle was in place, his spirit was free.

Shalom we called him. A prince of piece who touched in a special way everyone with whom he came in contact. He was a dog of Siberian Husky/German Shepherd mix and the owl called his name.

New Sailors of the Seas

Through the mist
a mast is seen
A ship ...
bringing new sailors of the sea.

Their songs and dances
are the sounds and movements
which connect us
through time and space.

Like dolphin and whale
their kindred in the sea
Their play is their truth,
their music, a message
to be.

They are: forever windward bound
forever crew
forever family
in their journey through
eternity.

New sailors of the seas.

I do not seek another to feel complete
But,
To enjoy the reflection.